Did GOD FORSAKE JESUS On the Cross?

Uncovering the Treasure
of Jesus' Dying Words

Karla Oakley Anderson

Copyright © 2013 by Karla Oakley Anderson

Did God Forsake Jesus on the Cross?
by Karla Oakley Anderson

Printed in the United States of America

ISBN 9781626973220

All rights reserved solely by the author. The author guarantees all contents are original and do not infringe upon the legal rights of any other person or work. No part of this book may be reproduced in any form without the permission of the author. The views expressed in this book are not necessarily those of the publisher.

Unless otherwise indicated, Bible quotations are taken from the New International Version. Copyright © 1973, 1978, 1984 by Biblica, Inc.™ Used by permission. All rights reserved.

www.xulonpress.com

ACKNOWLEDGMENTS

As a woman teacher in the body of Christ, during my forty years of studying and researching the Word of God, I have occasionally encountered those who think women should be silent in the church. No one disagrees with this point more than my husband, Mario. For all the times you have stood up for me, I am forever grateful for your love and respect. I wouldn't want to do this life without you.

To my sons, Ryan and Johnnie, what unspeakable joy you are to me! Thank you for sharing your love, wisdom, and compassion with me and all those you know. You are the anointed men that the Lord promised you would be.

Mama, there is no one who has loved me and believed in me like you. The precious time you spent teaching me how to pray and trust the Lord is etched in my memory. But your lifelong sacrificial love has been the true example to me and my five younger siblings - Gordon, Kathy, Denise,

Don, and Jay. Who am I that I should be blessed with the best family on earth? How I wish Papa was here to open this book. We so loved discussing the Scriptures together.

Dick Hensley, you are the best of enduring friends and one who helps me laugh through any trial. Your ministry and friendship is priceless. Montegus and Beyonka, God went out of His way when He sent you to be my stepson and stepdaughter. I so cherish your love and respect. To Christi, my daughter in the Lord who realized the truth of Jesus' cry from the cross as we studied together, thank you for traveling this bittersweet road with me. Lisa and Jennifer, you have changed my life by hearing, believing, and bearing fruit in His name. Pam Gorman, your support, love and faith in me keeps me motivated. Thanks for living outside the box. To all the women disciples in our home groups, you inspire me!

I would be remiss if I did not pay tribute to all the wonderful folks at Xulon Press. For your tireless efforts and for taking on a project that most rejected, may God bless you richly!

Contents

Introduction: The Question ix

1. Treasures of Wisdom and Knowledge 15

2. The Conventional Route: God Forsook Jesus 23

3. Clues in the Verse 41

4. Clues in the Context 55

5. Clues from the Culture 63

6. Dying Words: Failure or Fulfillment? 78

7. The Cross from Jesus' Point of View: Psalm 22 84

8. Summary 95

Introduction

The Question

The question, simply put, is this: ***Did God forsake Jesus on the cross?***

The answer? Well, that depends on who you ask. And no matter who you ask, the answer has to be either "yes," "no," "not sure," or "what difference does it make?"

Ask a Christian pastor or minister and you will hear an emphatic YES. Why their certainty? I think it's because of their long-standing position taken from a small assortment of extrapolated scriptures. We will explore that subject later.

However, one Christian minister I posed the question to responded, "What difference does it make? What's the importance of discovering whether or not God forsook Jesus?"

When I asked the question in our Bible-study group, there were mixed responses. Some said that if Jesus actually asked that upsetting question, "My God, my God, why have you forsaken me?" then God *must* have forsaken Him, right? Others surmised that Jesus was speaking from his human emotion.

However, the saddest answer of all was when I asked a Jewish friend of mine the question and he said, "Yes, God forsook Jesus because Jesus was a false Messiah." He continued, "Jesus realized in the end that He was not the Messiah, and that's why He asked that question. God would never forsake the real Messiah." Oh, did I mention that my Jewish friend used to be a practicing Christian who studied the Scriptures religiously and after "realizing" that God indeed forsook Jesus converted to Judaism? He is now awaiting the *first* coming of the Messiah.

So I'd say the answer makes a BIG difference in a BIG way, but not because it affects our salvation. When we believe in Jesus as our Savior, we are sealed for eternity. The answer could, however, shape our relationship and trust if we wonder, *'What kind of God is that who turns His back on His dying Son?'* That's why the accuracy, or right dividing, of the written Word is of supreme importance. The beliefs we hold as doctrine form our relationship with

Introduction

the Father and with His Son.

Probably by now you've figured out that my answer to the question is NO. I do *not* believe that God forsook Jesus on the cross. I also realize that I am in the minority.

How did I reach my conclusion? My search started over fifteen years ago when I was asked to teach on one verse at Easter - Matthew 27:46 where Jesus cries out from the cross, "My God, my God, why have you forsaken me?" The longer I listened to others sermons and studied for the meaning, the more that verse troubled me. After all, this was Jesus speaking. Agonizing words to hear from anyone, but especially from Jesus, the one who trusted His Father as no one ever has or ever will. Certainly He was forsaken by many of His followers—even His most trusted disciples whom He called friends—but His heavenly Father as well? Why would God do that or need to do that, I wondered. If my son were dying, I know where I would be—right by his bedside. If God looked away, detaching or separating Himself from His Son's predicament, that is heartbreaking indeed. There has to be more to this story than meets the eye which led me to another question: what if there is a deeper, scriptural, more believable truth behind this verse?

Some might close the book now and not even consider this possibility. After all, this topic has become hard and fast "doctrine" and is particularly emotionally charged, I've found. Certainly no one has all the answers or possesses all wisdom, so God instructs us to ask for more. He promised to give His wisdom liberally to all who *ask*.

The real question then becomes... Is there more knowledge and understanding, a veritable treasure waiting to be discovered behind the question, 'Did God forsake Jesus on the cross'?

And if there is, don't you want to know it?

Dedicated to My First Love, Jesus

I'd rather have Jesus than silver or gold
I'd rather have Him than riches untold
I'd rather have Jesus than anything
This world affords today.

—Mrs. Rhea F. Miller, Lyrics
1894–1966
—George Beverly Shea, Composer
1909–

CHAPTER 1

Treasures of Wisdom and Knowledge

*My purpose is that they may be encouraged in heart and united in love, so that they may have **full riches of complete understanding**, in order that they may know the **mystery** of God, namely, **Christ**, in whom are hidden **all the treasures** of wisdom and knowledge. I tell you this so that no one may **deceive you with fine-sounding arguments.***

—Colossians 2:2–4, emphasis added

This study is a bona fide treasure hunt—a search for the "full riches of complete understanding," a wealth of the "wisdom and knowledge" that is hidden in Christ, a "mystery" of God waiting to be discovered by the diligent seeker.

Prior to the gold rush in 1848, a simple farmer found a few gold nuggets on his land in the Sacramento Valley in

California. When word first began to spread, some thought it to be just rumor, but by 1849, gold fever had set in, and one of the largest migrations in history began. Huge sacrifices were made in order to fund this grueling journey westward by those prospective gold miners called the "forty-niners." Thousands borrowed money, mortgaged their property, or spent their life savings to follow the gold. Because they had to leave their families behind, the women carried the burden of running the farm or business while solely caring for their children.

"Think not that I have come to destroy the law or the prophets. I am not come to destroy, but to FULFILL."

The men traveled by land, over uncharted territory through mountains and deserts, others making their way by sea, in search of the kind of treasure theretofore unheard of. Some were lucky enough to find gold, although others paid the ultimate price along the way—death.

These men didn't find golden nuggets simply lying around loose on the ground. They had to pay attention to clues more carefully, dig a little deeper, work a little harder and never give up. Only then did they find the precious treasure they were seeking. There were no rewards for laziness. So it is with truth – it is only discovered by the most diligent seeker. The Scriptures and their meaning are like a great gold mine, just packed with hidden and sometimes unexpected riches, but we must seek until we find. It takes something akin to gold fever, a hunger and thirst so profound that there should be no risk too great or sacrifice too small that would prevent us from 'following the gold.'

Sadly, most people believe that gold or money is the answer to all their problems—dreaming of winning a lottery, becoming rich and famous and enjoying the self-gratifying pleasures of this world for a lifetime. Isn't it obvious that Hollywood, masquerading as the ultimate American dream in all its glitter and gold, is only an illusion? Behind all the smoke and mirrors of the luxurious lifestyle images we find ourselves fascinated with, lies the wreckage of broken lives, bankruptcy, addiction, betrayals, insecurities, emptiness, and untimely deaths. Does money really solve their problems or cause them?

Jesus asked this important question: "What does it profit a man if he gains the whole world but loses his own soul?"[1] True followers of Jesus pursue the true riches of wisdom and understanding which are much more precious than silver or gold.

Preparing for the Expedition

The first step in any journey is the planning phase. Before we head out on our search for *spiritual* truth, our first step is prayer. Prayer must be mixed with humility, for we know that God resists the proud but gives grace to the humble. It is the Spirit within us, the Holy Spirit, who searches the deep things of God.

On the night before His crucifixion, Jesus told His disciples: "I have yet many things to say unto you, but ye cannot bear them now. Howbeit when he, the Spirit of truth, is come, he will *guide you into all truth*: for he shall not speak of himself; but whatsoever he shall hear, *that* shall he speak: and he will show you things to come. *He shall glorify me*: for he shall receive of mine, and shall show *it* unto you."[2]

Notice his words "guide you into all truth." I think every believer and student of the Scriptures would agree that the treasures of wisdom and knowledge that are hidden in Christ are inexhaustible. But Jesus promised that the Comforter, the Spirit of truth, given to all who believe in Him, would guide us—and that includes guiding us through the Holy Scriptures. Jesus also indicated that the Spirit of truth would glorify Him. Therein lies the measuring stick: if something does not glorify the Lord, then we are on the wrong path.

I've learned over the years that it is perfectly okay with God to ask questions—to inquire of the Lord for myself, not simply accepting everything that is taught or fed to me. Scripture encourages us to pray, ask and seek. Questioning something scriptural doesn't mean that you don't have faith or doubt the authority of the Scriptures. To the contrary, we

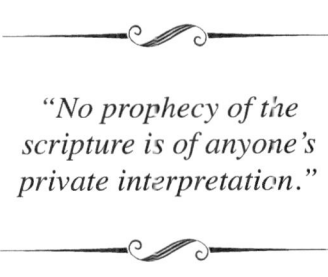

"No prophecy of the scripture is of anyone's private interpretation."

need the heart of a Berean, as mentioned in Acts 17:11: "These [Bereans] were more noble than those in Thessalonica, in that they received the word with all readiness of mind, and *searched the scriptures daily, whether those things were so"* [emphasis added).

Interpreting the Map of Scripture

If you are a teacher of God's Word, you are commanded to "study to show yourself approved unto God, a workman that needs *not to be ashamed*, rightly dividing the Word of Truth."[3] This verse indicates that it *is* possible to teach something that we should be ashamed about. The word *study* in Greek means "to put forth earnest and diligent effort; to strive with fervency." It is a serious matter to handle the Word of God. We must remember the Scripture's admonition that says, "Not many of you should presume to be teachers, because you know that we who teach will be judged more strictly."[4]

What a privilege to turn the pages of ancient Scripture kept largely uncontaminated through the centuries! But with any privilege comes responsibility. "Knowing this first, that no prophecy of the scripture is of anyone's private interpretation; for the word of God came not by the will of men, but holy men of God spoke as they were moved by the Holy Spirit."[5]

So how shall we proceed as we undertake such a daunting task without inserting our own personal interpretation or bias? One approach to hermeneutics, which is the theory of interpreting the Scriptures, is to view the Bible as mostly allegorical, full of metaphors and hyperbole, making an allowance for some of the miraculous events as symbolic or fables of life lessons.

It is true that the Scriptures contain figures of speech as well as shadows in the Old Testament that are illuminated in the New Testament. But Jesus Himself had an extremely high reverence for the Holy Scriptures, His life being resolutely based upon fulfilling them, saying in Matthew 5:17:

> "Think not that I have come to destroy the law or the prophets. I am not come to destroy, but to FULFILL" (emphasis added).

It would be difficult to exaggerate this very important declaration from the Son of God—that He came to fulfill the Scriptures. He added that "until heaven and earth pass, not one jot or one tittle[6] shall in no wise pass from the law until all be fulfilled." Jesus took a very serious, literal approach to His interpretation of the Scriptures, and in following suit, so should we.

The more literal approach to hermeneutics includes the following research tools, which we will use as our map:

1) VERSE: Does the verse interpret itself clearly in the verse? If not...
2) CONTEXT: Does the context in the immediate surrounding text or comparable texts make the meaning clearer?
3) CULTURE: Does the culture of the times and/or

Jewish history give us further understanding?

4) PREVIOUSLY EXPLAINED: Does the verse become clear in previous or other passages? Has it been used or explained before?

5) CONTRADICTIONS: Are there any contradictory scriptures?

6) DIALOGUE: Who is speaking, and who is being spoken to?

7) TRANSLATION: Does the meaning in the Hebrew or Greek give more clarity than the English translation?

8) SUM OF THE WORD: Is the whole counsel of God or the sum of the Word being taken into consideration?

Let's begin our journey now, prepared with prayer and equipped with our map of important research tools. I pray that by the time you see the wonders of the Scriptures unfold, you will gain a deeper amazement and adoration for the Savior Jesus Christ and His finest hour on earth!

CHAPTER 2

The Conventional Route: God Forsook Jesus

The secret things belong to the LORD our God, but the things revealed belong to us and to our children forever, that we may follow all the words of this law.
—DEUTERONOMY 29:29

After completing my studies in funeral education, I worked at a funeral home in Raleigh, North Carolina for three years serving at over 200 funerals. I heard the *why* question more times than I can count—from a mother who lost her child in miscarriage, from a lonely widower, whose world had revolved around his lovely wife of sixty years, from parents of a young military son, so proud of him and yet so brokenhearted. I heard *why* from the mothers of four young teenagers, just kids who had indulged in one too many drinks and flipped their car over a guardrail at 100 miles per hour, killing all four in an instant. I stood by many a graveside and cried with them for their loss. The question remained, why did this have to happen? Couldn't God have protected them? "Why did God forsake me?" they asked.

A Google search of these words *"My God, my God, why hast thou forsaken me?"* pulled up 810,000 results. YouTube posts over a thousand videos. This tells me that this verse is one of the most interesting and baffling ones in the Scriptures that intrigues scholars, students, and seekers alike. I reviewed hundreds of videos, and found that most were ideas that I had heard taught before, with maybe a few variations here and there.

What is the conventional route, the accepted doctrine, about this verse? The equation can be summed up like this:

A. Jesus became sin.

2 Corinthians 5: 21: "For he [God] hath made him [Jesus] *to be* sin for us, who knew no sin; that we might be made the righteousness of God in him." From this verse, the entire case is made that Jesus BECAME sin, even though "to be" is in italics in

the King James Version, indicating that those two words were added to the original text for clarity in translation.

I Peter 2:24: "He himself bore our sins in his body on the cross, so that we might die to sins and live for righteousness..."

B. God can't stand to look at sin.
Habakkuk 1:13: "Your [God's] eyes are too pure to look on [see] evil."

C. So if A = Jesus became sin, and B = God can't stand to look at sin, then C = God could not look at Jesus who became sin, but had to look away, forsaking His Son on the cross.

That's it in its simplest form. Some add that the reason that Jesus had to experience this unbearable separation or abandonment from His Father was for our sakes, so that we would never have to. In essence, Jesus endured the wrath of God in our place, suffering something even worse than the unthinkable horror of crucifixion—spiritual separation and abandonment from His Father.

Where does it say (chapter and verse, please) that

Jesus needed to endure a single moment of His Father's abandonment and separation from Him in order that we would never have to? What made our salvation complete—the so-called abandonment from the Father or His perfect blood sacrifice? Wasn't death for three days and three nights separation enough?

What is it that keeps us clinging to the notion that God forsook His Son? And yet, Easter after Easter, the painful points are reiterated. One author puts it this way:

> "It is possible that at some moment on the cross, when Jesus became sin on our behalf, that God the Father, in a sense, turned His back upon the Son. It says in Habakkuk 1:13 that God is too pure to look upon evil. Therefore, it is possible that when Jesus bore our sins in His body on the cross, that the Father, spiritually, turned away. At that time, the Son may have cried out. One thing is for sure. We have no capacity to appreciate the utterly horrific experience of having the sins of the world put upon the Lord Jesus as He hung, in excruciating pain, from that cross. The physical pain was immense. The spiritual one must have been even greater."[1]

Another minister writes:

> "In those awful moments, Jesus was expressing His feelings of abandonment as God placed the sins of the world on Him—and because of that God had to 'turn away' from Jesus. As Jesus was feeling that weight of sin, He was experiencing separation from God for the only time in all of eternity. It was at this time that 2 Corinthians 5:21 occurred, 'God made Him who had no sin to be sin for us, so that in Him we might become the righteousness of God.' Jesus became sin for us, so He felt the loneliness and abandonment that sin always produces, except that in His case, it was not His sin—it was ours.[2]

A lesser-used explanation is that Christ spoke these words out of His humanity—that as a human being with feelings, He expressed what someone in pain and anguish might voice, like the 'whys' I heard at the funeral home. Subsequently, this becomes a rhetorical question; it assumes that God *did* forsake Jesus simply because Jesus asked the question.

There's more ambiguity. Exactly how long did God forsake Jesus? Jesus uttered seven sentences from the cross over a period of about six hours. Jesus first spoke to His Father, saying, "Father, forgive them for they know not what they do." Okay, so He was speaking to God there, so He hadn't been forsaken yet. Next, Jesus spoke to the thief, telling him that he would be in paradise. Then, He spoke to John and His mother, and later, He expressed His thirst. Finally, He cried out with a loud voice, asking God why He had been forsaken. So did the forsaking happen right after He asked the Father to forgive His perpetrators and then end when He spoke to his Father again, saying, "Father, into thy hands I commit my spirit"? What would you estimate? Was the abandonment for maybe three or four hours? Was it less? Was it more?

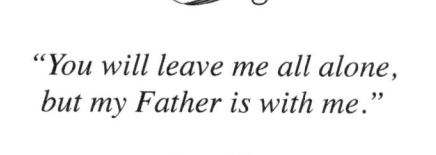

"You will leave me all alone, but my Father is with me."

Consider these words spoken by Jesus just hours before His crucifixion: "Do you think I cannot call on my Father, and he will at once put at my disposal more than twelve legions of angels? But how then would the Scriptures be fulfilled that say it must happen this way?"[3] Was there a time limit placed on this guarantee — that angels, sent by the Father, would rush to his aid? Would it include the time Jesus was on the cross?

"But a time is coming, and in fact has come, when you will be scattered, each to his own home. You will leave me all alone, but *my Father is with me.*" [4]

Do these confessions from Jesus sound like a man soon to be forsaken by His Father? Of course not. "When they hurled their insults at him, he did not retaliate; when he suffered, he made no threats. Instead, he entrusted himself to him who judges justly."[5] Here's a good question: how do you entrust yourself to someone who has abandoned you?

I'm certainly not criticizing anyone who has believed or taught that God forsook Jesus, for we all know in part. We have blindly accepted these sermons handed down to us, which use three or four proof texts (some *out* of context) to deal with this disturbing enigma. I understand. Looking at this verse in the twenty-first century simply at face value, while holding a deep-rooted image of an angry God against sinful man, one might accept this explanation. But you will see, after the truth is revealed about Jesus' cry from the cross, just how awfully distorted, cruel, and misleading this explanation is.

So you get the idea. It makes for a very captivating story, vividly demonstrating the wrath of God against mankind's sin taken out on Jesus. But herein lies the dilemma: if this conventional route indeed is a right dividing of the Scriptures, then there are some very egregious implications.

Did Jesus BECOME sin? What does that mean?

Webster's Dictionary translates the word "become" as "to evolve into." Synonyms include the following: "assume the form of, be converted into, to be transformed into, change into, emerge as, to grow into, to metamorphose or turn into."

Since we know that Jesus was a sinless man, what exactly could it mean that He "became" sin? Did He evolve into, was converted into, or was transformed into the personification of sin? Of course not. He could not BE SIN and BE SINLESS at the same time—especially in the same sentence! Otherwise, you have a grammatical antithesis or some kind of mystical meaning.

So, to be thorough, let's look at a few other verses with similar concepts. First Peter 2:24 says, "He himself bore our sins in his body on the tree, so that we might die to sins and live for righteousness; by his wounds you have been healed."

The *Bible in Basic English* translates it this way: "He

took our sins on himself, giving his body to be nailed on the tree, so that we, being dead to sin, might have a new life in righteousness, and by his wounds we have been made well."

Romans 8:3–4 in the King James Version reads, " For what the law could not do, in that it was weak through the flesh, God sending his own Son in the likeness of sinful flesh, and for sin, condemned sin in the flesh: That the righteousness of the law might be fulfilled in us."

Note the word "offering" or "sacrifice" in other translations of those same two verses in Romans:

- *New International Version:* "For what the law was powerless to do because it was weakened by the flesh, God did by sending his own Son in the likeness of sinful flesh to be a sin offering. And so he condemned sin in the flesh."
- *New Living Translation:* "He sent his own Son in a body like the bodies we sinners have. And in that body God declared an end to sin's control over us by giving his Son as a sacrifice for our sins."
- *The Holman Christian Standard Bible*: "What the law could not do since it was limited by the flesh, God did. He condemned sin in the flesh by sending

His own Son in flesh like ours under sin's domain, and as a sin offering."
- *New Century Version*: "The law was without power, because the law was made weak by our sinful selves. But God did what the law could not do. He sent his own Son to earth with the same human life that others use for sin. By sending his Son to be an offering for sin, God used a human life to destroy sin."

Similarly, consider these verses in Hebrews:
- Hebrews 10:12: "But this man, after he had offered one sacrifice for sins forever, sat down on the right hand of God."
- Hebrews 9:13-14, 27-28: "For if the blood of goats and bulls, and the sprinkling of defiled persons with the ashes of a heifer, sanctify for the purification of the flesh, how much more will the blood of Christ, who through the eternal Spirit offered himself without blemish to God, purify our conscience from dead works to serve the living God. ... And just as it is appointed for man to die once, and after that comes judgment, so Christ, having been offered once to bear the sins of many, will

appear a second time, not to deal with sin but to save those who are eagerly waiting for him."

Okay. I think the point is made. Suffice it to say that the aforementioned scriptures depict Jesus as an offering or sacrifice for sin. We will discuss this further in chapter 4.

Are God's Eyes Too Pure to Look on Evil?

If God can't stand to look at sin, then how can He judge it or forgive it? The account of Noah is a perfect example of God actually looking at sin. Genesis 6:5 records, "The Lord saw that the wickedness of humankind was great in the earth", and verse 11 states, "Now the earth was corrupt in God's sight and was full of violence." Obviously, God can see sin. If He couldn't, how did He know to cover Adam and Eve's sin? Cain sinned, and God not only saw it, but He had mercy on him. God is not blind to sin. After all, God so loved the world, which is full of sinful people.

Yet Habakkuk 1:13 does say just that: 'Your eyes are too pure to look on evil." But we must ask ourselves: who is speaking, and to whom are they speaking? A closer look at the context of this verse is of paramount importance. The first verse of chapter 1 begins with the prophet

Habakkuk's complaint to God about how much evil there was and asking Him when He would do something about it. Habakkuk cried out to God, saying,

Habakkuk 1:2, 3: "How long, O Lord, must I call for help, but you do not listen? Or cry out to you, 'Violence!' but you do not save? Why do you make me look at injustice? Why do you tolerate wrong? Destruction and violence are before me; there is strife, and conflict abounds."

God gives to Habakkuk this alarming reply:

Habakkuk 1:5 – 7, 9: "Look at the nations and pay attention! You will be shocked and amazed! For I will do something in your lifetime that you would not believe even if you were told.

Look, I am about to empower the Babylonians, that ruthless and greedy nation. They sweep across the surface of the earth, seizing dwelling places that do not belong to them.

They are frightening and terrifying; they decide for themselves what is right.

All of them intend to do violence."

God was not only seeing the evil of the villainous Babylonians; He was going to empower them to bring judgment against Israel! Habakkuk was shocked and completely perplexed. How could God not only tolerate evil, but also use evil to bring about His judgment?

Watch as Habakkuk wrestled with God, bargaining for another option:

> Habakkuk 1:12, 13: "O Lord, are you not from everlasting? My God, my Holy One, we will not die. Lord, you have appointed them [the Babylonians] as your instrument of judgment. O Rock, You have appointed them as your instrument of punishment." You can almost hear Habakkuk's tone of incredulity. So then he pleads, **"Your eyes are too pure to look on evil; you cannot tolerate wrong.** So why do you put up with such treacherous people? Why are you silent while the wicked devour those more righteous than they are?" (emphasis added).

God did not say His eyes were too pure to look on evil. Habakkuk did. In fact, just the opposite is declared by God. One minister told me that even though Habakkuk said,

"Your eyes are too pure to look at evil," that this verse is Scripture and we should not say that Scripture is wrong. I am not saying that Scripture is wrong—Habakkuk was. He was saying something that does not apply to our omniscient God Almighty!

There are other accounts of men not understanding God's plan, such as Job's miserable comforters, whom God handled by saying: "I am angry with you and your two friends, because *you have not spoken of me what is right*, as my servant Job has."[6]

Think about this. The third commandment states: "Thou shalt not take the name of the Lord in vain, for the LORD will not hold him guiltless that taketh his name in vain."[7] The Hebrew word for *vain*[8] means "emptiness, deceitful, or false." Whenever we speak of God that which is not true of Him, we are speaking His name in vain, essentially breaking the third commandment. To be sure, taking the Lord's name in vain means much more than using His name with vulgar language.

Habakkuk was soliciting a different solution than what God had planned. But God would not be moved. He insisted that He would use the unrighteous to further His will. Even though Habakkuk was stunned, God assured him that eventually the corrupt Babylonians would be destroyed.

This was an intense dialogue between God and Habakkuk, and perhaps a difficult concept for Habakkuk to grasp. But God had done this before – used evil for good, so to speak. God saw the evil in Lucifer's heart when pride was found in him. Because God could *see* the evil, He cast Lucifer and a third of the fallen angels to the earth. In the book of Job, the very first book of the Bible to be written, we are told that Satan destroyed all that Job possessed, including his children—and God allowed it. But eventually God's justice was done, and all that Job lost was restored *doubly*. Then there is the account of Joseph when, as a boy, he was traded as a slave by his own brothers; but as a man, he became the redemptive source for Israel during the worldwide famine. Joseph told his brothers that what the devil meant for harm, God used for good.

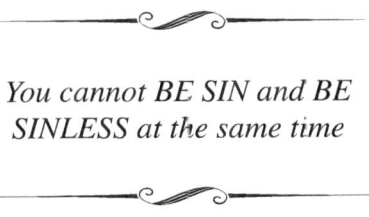

You cannot BE SIN and BE SINLESS at the same time

But none of these tops Jesus' Garden of Gethsemane experience: "If it be possible, let this cup pass from Me; nevertheless, not as I will, but as Thou wilt."[9] As the hateful and evil Romans and Pharisees determined to crucify the Son of God, God used that evil to accomplish the greatest of all good—the salvation of mankind!

God's ways are higher than man's ways and His thoughts higher than our thoughts. His judgments are unsearchable and His ways past finding out. But the Scriptures are clear that God sometimes allows, even uses, evil to bring to pass His ultimate purpose. So it is silly to say that God cannot see evil, or to use Habakkuk's statement as a foundational premise for theological doctrine.

Was Jesus the Misunderstood Martyr?

Another troubling implication of the conventionally accepted teaching concerns what we could call the "martyrdom of Jesus." In the Old Testament and all throughout the history of the church, there have been scores of martyrs who went quietly and courageously to their deaths, knowing that God was with them. It seems so uncharacteristic and irrational that Jesus, the Son of God obeying His Father's request, would whimper and mutter that terrifying question. Could this be the cry of a mere mortal's emotions of fear, doubt, and defeat crying out as a misunderstood martyr?

I can't buy that. Right before the actual crucifixion, Jesus crucified His own flesh in the Garden of Gethsemane.

He knew the torturous suffering that lay ahead of Him. He knew the devil would glory in His death. The distress He felt as he prayed through His tears mingled with blood was the most earnest of all prayers ever uttered. He asked His Father to let this cup pass from Him. But something must have happened in the garden to strengthen him, just as it did when Jesus was in the wilderness facing the devil himself.

Hebrews 12: 2 says, "Let us fix our eyes on Jesus, the author and finisher of our faith, who, for the joy that was set before him (and who gave him that joy? It had to be the Father], endured the cross, despising [disregarding] its shame."

Astonishing! Jesus disregarded the shame because of the joy that was set before Him while He endured the cross! What in heaven's name was the joy that He experienced? Whatever it was, it was enough to make the cross worth all the suffering. It is quite possible that Jesus could have seen our faces—the ones who would believe on His name—as the fulfillment of what He was accomplishing through His suffering. After all, He did pray for you before He was arrested. "My prayer is not for them alone. I pray also for those who will believe in me through their message, that all of them may be one, Father, just as you are in me and I am in you." [10]

Isaiah 50: 7 says that He "set His face like flint"; and He got up with courage provoked by love when He spoke, "Nevertheless, not My will, but Yours be done." Jesus was no coward. His cry on the cross was not prompted by human weakness, and as you will see, anything but!

I now pose this question: is the conventional teaching that God forsook Jesus satisfactory for you? Do you find the "research" a bit careless, containing a few contradictions and gaps?

I believe that the aforementioned systematic research principles must be applied to uncover more possibilities, and that's exactly where we go in our next chapter.

CHAPTER 3

CLUES IN THE VERSE

From the sixth hour until the ninth hour, darkness came over all the land. About the ninth hour, Jesus cried out in a loud voice, "Eloi, Eloi, lama sabachthani?" which means, "My God, My God, why hast thou forsaken me?"
—MATTHEW 27:46

*E*ven a new student to the Bible will discover that most verses are clear just as they are written; in other words, the verse interprets itself. Matthew 27:46 is not one of those. There are apparent inconsistencies in these nine words. Let's look at each of them.

GREEK to Me

My first question is, why did the translators, or Matthew and Mark, leave the words *'Eloi, Eloi, lama sabachthani'* in the text? This verse stands out like a sore thumb.

Matthew and Mark deliberately wrote this transliteration of the Greek in their gospels, which was the common language at that time. They seemed to be going out of their way to make sure that their Greek readers understood that Jesus was actually quoting Scripture when He said these words. But any devout Jew would have immediately recognized Jesus' cry as a direct quote of Psalm 22 since it had always been acknowledged as an important and well known Messianic psalm. Today, most Christians know the twenty-third psalm by heart, but the Jews knew Psalm 22, 23 and 24 from memory and considered these a Messianic trilogy. More on that point later.

"MY GOD, MY GOD"

First of all, Jesus very rarely referred to His Father as "God" or "My God." He consistently spoke of and to His "Father." He taught His disciples, when praying the Lord's

Prayer, to say "Our Father." On the few occasions that He used the word *God*, it is the Greek word *theos*[1] throughout the Gospels. In Matthew 22:37, Jesus said the greatest commandment was to "love the Lord your God," and frequently He spoke of the kingdom of God. After His resurrection, He said to Mary Magdalene, "Touch me not; for I am not yet ascended to my Father: but go to my brethren, and say unto them, I ascend unto my Father, and your Father; and to my God, and your God.' "[2]

It is important to note, however, that from the cross, Jesus used the word 'Father' twice: "Father, forgive them," and "Father, into your hands I commit my spirit." So crying out "My God, My God" gives us reason to pause. It was unquestionably out of character for Jesus.

"WHY"

Unless the word *'why'* is used to open a rhetorical question, then the definition is "a question concerning the cause or reason for which something is done, i.e., not understanding something."[3] Now stop and think about this. Did Jesus not understand what was happening that day on the cross?

Certainly that's not the case because Jesus knew that

His mission and purpose was to die for the sins of the world when He said, "Now my heart is troubled, and what shall I say? 'Father, save me from this hour'? No, it was for this very reason I came to this hour."[4]

"I came from the Father and entered the world; now I am leaving the world and going back to the Father."[5] "I love the Father and I do exactly what my Father has commanded me."[6] When Peter drew his sword and struck the high priest's servant, Jesus said to Peter, "Shall I not drink the cup the Father has given me?"[7] And again, "Jesus, knowing all that was going to happen to Him, went out and asked them, 'Who is it you want?'"[8]

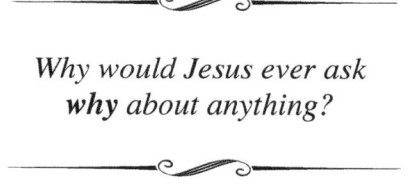

*Why would Jesus ever ask **why** about anything?*

Do you remember what Moses and Elijah discussed with Jesus during His transfiguration? "[Jesus] took with him Peter and John and James and went up on the mountain to pray. And as he was praying, the appearance of his face was altered, and his clothing became dazzling white. And behold, two men were talking with him, Moses and Elijah, who appeared in glory and spoke of his departure which he was about to accomplish at Jerusalem."[9] A few verses later, we are told, "As the time approached for him to be taken up to heaven, Jesus resolutely set out for Jerusalem." He knew everything that was going to occur. There was no need for Him to ask when, where, what, how or why!

In fact, why would Jesus ever ask *why* about anything? "Why have you forsaken me?" could indicate at best, not understanding the will of God, or at worst, suspicion or doubt—as if to say incredulously, "How could you abandon me now?" Jesus scolded Peter for his doubt when Jesus rescued him from the water: "Immediately Jesus reached out his hand and caught him, saying to him, 'You of little faith, why did you doubt?'"[10] Just before His crucifixion, Jesus explained to Peter, "Simon, Simon, Satan has asked to sift you as wheat. But I have prayed for you, Simon that your faith may not fail. And when you have turned back, strengthen your brothers."[11] When Jesus rebuked His disciples for doubting God, or having little faith, it was because doubting God meant not trusting Him, and doubting equals sin, correct?

Did Jesus have little faith, or doubt, when He asked '*why*'? If He did and expressed His doubt, then He sinned in the final hour. You see my point. This presents a major problem, for the Scriptures unequivocally teach that Jesus was sinless.[12] The Lamb of God had to be a perfect sacrifice, without spot or blemish. Doubting would make Jesus imperfect, which would render us unsaved. It would also mean that Jesus duplicated what Adam and Eve did when tempted, which was to doubt that God had their best interest at heart and harbor suspicion of His goodness. Sadly, it would be a repeat of the original sin and the subsequent fall of man.

"FORSAKEN"

Psalm 9:10 emphatically states, "And they that know thy name will put their trust in thee: For thou, LORD, hast not forsaken them that seek thee." I believe Jesus undoubtedly falls into this category.

God stood by His faithful prophets, saying to Moses, "Be strong and courageous. Do not be afraid or terrified because of them [their enemies], for the Lord your God goes with you; He will never leave you, nor forsake you."[13] And to Joshua, He spoke, "As I was with Moses, so I will be with you; I will never leave you nor forsake you." [14]

If God can't stand to look at sin, why did He promise never to abandon Moses or Joshua, who certainly were not sinless? Jesus knew the promises made to these men of God; therefore, He had to know that His Father would never forsake Him either.

Why would Jesus think God had forsaken Him if He knew and believed the prophetic scriptures concerning His life and destiny? Hadn't the Father spoken on at least two occasions, "This is my beloved Son in whom I am well pleased"? Wasn't Jesus doing the will of His Father when He laid down His life for us? He absolutely was. Consequently, it is imperative that we ask the next question:

Does God Forsake His Own?

At times in history, yes, the Lord God does exhibit an abandonment type of wrath towards individuals and nations, but keep in mind that this is only after they have forsaken Him. Psalm 81:10 explains how this abandonment occurs: "I am the LORD your God, who brought you up out of Egypt. Open wide your mouth and I will fill it. But my people would not listen to me; Israel would not submit to me. So I gave them over to their stubborn hearts to follow their own devices."

The apostle Paul makes it clear in Romans 1:18 that "the wrath of God is being revealed against all the godlessness and wickedness of men who suppress the truth." How? In verse 26, it says that God "gave them over," which is the Greek word *paradidómi*, meaning, "to hand over, to give or deliver over, to abandon." God does not interfere with or manipulate anyone's free will. So those who choose to make a continued practice of wickedness and idolatry incur the consequences, or reap what they sow. The good news is that when anyone or any nation repents, turns to the Lord and gives up their defiance, God can then intervene, pouring out His forgiveness and healing.

Let's look at a few instances in the Old Testament that speak of God forsaking His people, Israel, but please note that in each instance, Israel had *first* forsaken God and turned to idols.

- Deuteronomy 31:16–17: Speaking of Israel's rebellion, the Lord spoke to Moses, saying: "They will forsake Me and break the covenant I made with them. On that day, I will become angry with them and forsake them; I will hide my face from them, and they will be destroyed."

- 2 Kings 21:12–15: After King Manasseh's detestable practices of the occult and teaching Israel his evil ways, God spoke: "I will forsake the remnant of my inheritance and hand them over to their enemies ... because they have done evil in my eyes and have provoked me to anger" (I suppose that means He could "see" their evil).

- Isaiah 59:1–3: "Behold, the LORD's hand is not shortened, that it cannot save, or his ear dull, that it cannot hear; but your iniquities have made a separation between you and your God, and your sins have hidden his face from you so that he does not hear. For your hands are stained with blood, your fingers with guilt. Your lips have spoken falsely, and your tongue mutters wicked things."

- Jeremiah 2:17 and 19 says, "You have brought all this on yourself, Israel, by forsaking the Lord your God when he was leading you along the right path. . . . Your wickedness will punish you; your backsliding will rebuke you. Consider then and realize how evil and bitter it is for you when you forsake the Lord your God and have no awe of me."

- In Jeremiah 23, the entire chapter is devoted to God's anger regarding the false prophets and shepherds who were doing flagrant damage to God's people. They were abusing their authority, neglecting the people's needs, and taking the name of the Lord in vain. In verses 33 and 39, God spoke to them: "I will forsake you, declares the Lord. If a prophet or a priest or anyone else claims, 'This is the oracle of the Lord,' I will punish that man and his household. . . . Therefore, I will surely forget you and cast you out of my presence." God does not like it when his so-called leaders speak falsely in His name and do not care for His flock.

- The first three chapters of Hosea indicate that the Lord kept calling Israel back to His love. God told Hosea to marry a prostitute. She repeatedly strayed from him, returned to her evil ways, and was unfaithful to her husband. Yet Hosea was instructed by the Lord to search for her and bring her back and treat her tenderly. This was to be an example to Israel of how much the Lord loved them even after they continued to return to their former evil ways, whoring after other gods. However, chapters 4–14 clearly show that Israel was not willing to give up her idols, but pursued a spirit of prostitution. So in Hosea 10:17, Hosea announced that "my God will reject them, because they have not obeyed him."

Let's make this perfectly clear: when God 'forsook,' He was simply allowing disobedience and evil practices to reap their poisonous consequences. But there is another side to this. There are hundreds of instances where God's people forsook *Him,* yet in His great mercy and grace, He still would *not* forsake them! Even now, we may run away from God, but He never hides His face from us. When we as sons and daughters are practicing sinful ways, our fellowship is broken relationally, but *never* positionally. When we confess our sins, repent and draw near to Him, He restores us and cleanses us of all unrighteousness all because of the love and sacrifice of Jesus. Now, by His blood, nothing—not even death—can separate us from the love of God.

> *It was Israel's sins that separated them from God*

"With a LOUD Voice"

Matthew 27:46 and Mark 15:33 both indicate that Jesus cried out "My God, my God, why hast thou forsaken me?" with a LOUD voice. Can you imagine after all the brutal beatings and length of time on the cross that He could shout with a loud voice, when His strength should have been dried up? We don't have the privilege of hearing Jesus' tone or the inflection in His voice. Just as in a letter, email or text, the meaning might be clouded if you cannot see or hear the person speaking and miscommunication sometimes results. So it is with this cry of Jesus. The one thing that is distinctively unambiguous is that this question was not muttered. It was a cry so loud that He may have deliberately wanted these words heard clearly.

This was not the first instance of Jesus crying out with a loud voice. "During his earthly life Christ offered both requests and supplications, with loud cries and tears, to the one who was able to save him from death and he was heard because of his devotion."[15]

Jesus cried out to the Father with loud cries and tears, as He did in the Garden of Gethsemane, and He was heard! Who heard Him? The Father who was able to deliver Him from death!

There is another mention of Jesus crying out with a loud voice, and that was when He stood at the tomb of Lazarus, a friend He loved dearly. He first prayed, "Father, I thank you that you have heard me. I know that you always hear me, but I said this for the people standing here, that they may believe you sent me." When He had said this, Jesus called in a loud voice, "Lazarus, come forth!" [16] So *why* did Jesus call out loudly? So that those around would hear and believe! Believe what? That God had sent Him!

Interestingly, Jesus also cried with a loud voice His final words before He died: "Father, into Your hands I commit my spirit."[17]

There are also several references to a "loud voice" in the book of Revelation. Angels and large throngs in heaven cry out with a loud voice. And so does Jesus, the Christ, the Messiah, the King of Kings and Lord of Lords! John writes:

Revelation 1:10: "I was in the Spirit on the Lord's Day when I heard behind me a loud voice like a trumpet."

Revelation 11:12 "Then they [the two witnesses that had been dead] heard a loud voice from heaven saying to them: 'Come up here!' So the two prophets went up to heaven in a cloud while their enemies stared at them."

Revelation 21:3: "And I heard a loud voice from the throne saying: 'Look! The dwelling of God is with men. He will live among them, and they will be his people, and God himself will be with them.'"

It seems that when a loud voice is used, we need to pay attention! The fact that Jesus cried out this question, "My God, my God, why hast thou forsaken me?" with a loud voice must have tremendous significance. As in the case with Lazarus, *what did He want us to believe?*

The answer will astound you!

CHAPTER 4

Clues in the Context

"The sum of your word is truth, and every one of your righteous laws endures forever."
—PSALM 119:60

If you watch the news at all, you'll hear tidbits, or sound bites, from a politician's speech or a clip of a few words the president has spoken. Many times that's all we get—a snippet. As a result, our opinions are formed based on a small phrase that someone spoke. Without listening to the entire speech or at least the surrounding material, it is almost impossible to get the full meaning or intention behind it.

Knowing the context is elementary in biblical research. The full context

The sum of Your Word is truth

can give us much more to go on when interpreting a single verse. For instance, you could say that the Bible itself declares "there is no God." But if you read the entire phrase of Psalm 53:1, it says, "The fool has said in his heart, 'There is no God.'" Because the Word of God is living, anyone can make it say almost anything IF it is taken out of context. Accurately interpreting the Word of God is dependent on having an overall knowledge of the Scriptures so that just sound bites are not taken to express or even possibly distort its true meaning.

Jesus *is* the WORD, and He chose His words very carefully. When facing the devil directly during His forty-day-long wilderness suffering, the only words recorded that He spoke to the devil were "it is written" followed by Scripture.[1] Isn't it odd how the devil also knew and quoted the Word of God? BUT the important difference was, the devil twisted its meaning by taking it out of context. If our enemy knows the Scriptures, maybe we should too—but in context!

Evaluating the context surrounding the cry that Jesus made from the cross is our next step, since the meaning of Matthew 27:46 is not clear in the verse alone. Reading Matthew 27, we basically see the events of the crucifixion unfold as follows:

The soldiers took Jesus into the Praetorian, stripped him, put a scarlet robe on him, and then placed a crown of thorns on his head. Placing a staff in his Jesus' hand, they knelt in front of him and mocked him by saying, 'Hail, King of the Jews!' They spit on him, took the staff and struck him on the head again and again. Then they led him away to crucify him. As they were going out, they met a man from Cyrene, named Simon, whom they forced to help carry the cross.

Everything that was happening to Jesus was so that Scripture would be fulfilled.

When they had crucified Jesus, they divided up his clothes by casting lots and kept watch over him. Above his head they placed the written charge against him: 'This is Jesus, the King of the Jews.' Two robbers were crucified with him, one on either side of him. Those who passed by hurled insults at him, saying, 'You who are going to destroy the temple and build it in three days, save yourself! Come down from the cross, if you are the Son of God!'

The chief priests and the elders taunted and mocked him too—'He saved others, but he can't save himself! He's the King of Israel! Let him come down now from the cross, and we will believe in him. He trusts in God. Let

God rescue him now if He wants him, for he said, 'I am the Son of God.'

Then, from 3:00 – 6:00 in the afternoon, an ominous thick darkness covered the land. "About the ninth hour Jesus cried out in a loud voice, *"Eloi, Eloi, lama sabachthani?"*—which means, 'My God, my God, why have you forsaken me?'"

Continuing in the context following that verse, some of those standing near said that He was calling for Elijah. Someone ran and got a sponge, filled it with wine vinegar, put it on a stick, and offered it to Jesus to drink. Others said to leave Him alone and see if Elijah would come to save him. Afterward, Jesus gave up his spirit.

The immediate context in Matthew 27 tells of the process and events as they unfolded. However, there seems to be no real clue here that would explain what Jesus meant by the looming question. Subsequently, the next step in considering the context is to look at the comparable texts from the Gospel of Luke and the Gospel of John (Mark's gospel repeats some of the same information, so we will not include it here).

Comparing the Context in the Gospels of Luke and John

John, the beloved disciple and part of the inner circle of three, was the only one of the twelve who was present at the cross when Jesus was dying. Jesus must have thought very highly of John, since He entrusted the care of His mother to him.

Watch closely as you read John's gospel, for he seems intently focused on showing the reader that everything happening to Jesus was so that **Scripture would be fulfilled.** And if that is the case – that Scripture was being fulfilled—it would **prove that Jesus was the Messiah,** which meant that **we could believe in Him.**

Before His crucifixion, Jesus stressed this point several times with His disciples:

- "But this is to **fulfill the scripture**: 'He who shares my bread has lifted up his heel against me. I am telling you now *before* it happens, so that when it *does* happen, *you will believe* that I am He [the Messiah]."[2]
- "I have told you now before it happens, so that

when it does happen, *you will believe."*[3]

- "But this is to **fulfill** what is written in their Law: 'They hated me without reason.' "[4]
- "When the soldiers crucified Jesus, they took his garments, dividing them into four shares, one for each of them with the undergarment remaining. This garment was seamless, woven in one piece from top to bottom. 'Let's not tear it,' they said to one another. 'Let's cast lots for it.' This happened *that the scripture might be fulfilled*, which said, 'They divided my garments among them and cast lots for my clothing.' "[5]
- "Later, knowing that all was now completed, and so *that the scripture would be fulfilled*, Jesus said, 'I thirst.' "[6]
- "But when they came to Jesus and found that he was already dead, they did not break his legs. Instead, one of the soldiers pierced Jesus' side with a spear, bringing a sudden flow of blood and water. The man who saw it has given testimony, and his testimony is true. He knows that he tells the truth, and he testifies *so that you also may believe.* These things happened *so that the scripture would be fulfilled:*[7] 'Not one of his bones will

be broken,'[8] and, as **another scripture says**, 'They will look on the one they have pierced.' "[9]

- "Jesus said to his disciples just prior to his arrest, 'It is written: "And he was numbered with the transgressors";[10] and I tell you that **this must be fulfilled in me. Yes, what is written about me is reaching its fulfillment.'** "[11]

Can you see the startling pattern of what is unfolding? Scriptures written hundreds, even thousands, of years before Christ was born were coming to the climax of completion, but no one seemed to know it at the time except for our precious Savior!

Forgive me if I am belaboring this point, but it is empirically clear that Jesus was fulfilling Scripture beginning with his birth all the way through to his death. You might ask 'what difference does that make?' Here's the answer: only one man could do that — the promised Messiah, the very Son of God and Son of Man. That is precisely why we can believe in Him!

Could Jesus' cry from the cross be a fulfillment of Scripture?

Consequently, the next most reasonable question is:

Could Jesus' cry from the cross that day possibly be a fulfillment of Scripture as well?

We can't give up the search now. We are so close to the answer!

CHAPTER 5

Clues from the Culture

For whatsoever things were written aforetime were written for our learning, that we through patience and comfort of the scriptures might have hope.

—ROMANS 15:4

Without a reasonable doubt, the jury is still out concerning the verse or the context. We must journey back in time to examine the Jewish culture of the day; however, we cannot view it properly through twenty-first-century eyes.

As Saint Augustine said, the Old Testament is the New Testament concealed and the New Testament is the Old Testament revealed. Without an understanding of the Old, the New will remain clouded to us. For example, Hebrews 11, sometimes referred to as the "hall of faith," speaks of great men and women who changed the world by their righteous stand.

If you were fortunate to be raised in a Christian home, as I was, you probably learned the miraculous stories of Noah's ark, David and Goliath, Daniel in the lions' den, Shadrach, Meshach, and Abednego in the fiery furnace and so on. However, as adults, we tend to pay very little attention to the Old Testament anymore. Some say it is too scary, or the bizarre incidents seem unrealistic. Since I did not understand the Jewish roots belonging to Christianity, it took me many years of studying before I ever connected the Old Testament with the New. As Dr. Chuck Missler is fondly quoted as saying:

> "The Bible is an integrated message system, made of 66 books and penned by over 40 authors. The Old Testament tells history in reverse. There are over 8000 prophecies proven to be written hundreds even thousands of years before Christ that specifically point to his birth, life, suffering, death, resurrection, glory and the Kingdom of God. There is no other prophet of any religion who had as many prophecies foretold and fulfilled than Jesus Christ. He is the central theme of every book in

the Old Testament and the first promise that He would come is in Genesis 3:15! Understanding the Old Testament is paramount to fitting the puzzle pieces of the New Testament. The Old Testament is filled with so many events, prophecies, promises, clues to what was to come and is to come that it would take more than a lifetime to uncover all the treasures."[1]

Remember, the Old Testament scriptures were all that Jesus had and, of course, all He quoted from. Every book in the Old Testament was completed and compiled before Jesus' life on earth.[2] Apparently He had no problem with its historical and prophetic accounts or which books were canonized, thereby authenticating it.

TRADITION IN JEWISH CULTURE

Let's look at some of the facts concerning Jewish culture and religion at the time Jesus lived:

1) The Old Testament was written on parchment-type scrolls held in the temple, so there were no Bibles, and the Jewish people did not have their

own copies to read or study. Therefore, the Jewish community spent time learning and memorizing the Scriptures because they knew that it was the divine revelation of God. Jewish men and young boys, ages five and up, studied with rabbis and, with tremendous dedication and toil, were expected to memorize Scripture and teach their families. This oral tradition was passed from each generation to the next.[3]

2) As a means of rehearsing the scriptures, or during times of worship, the Rabbi would quote the first line or sentence of a scriptural section and then the congregation would follow by quoting the rest from memory. Lastly, the Rabbi closed with the last verse of the section.

So important was the memorization of Scripture that the Lord God spoke these words in Deuteronomy 6:4–9:

"Hear, O Israel: The Lord our God, the Lord is one. Love the Lord your God with all your heart and with all your soul and with all your strength. These commandments that I give you today are to be upon your hearts. Impress them on your children. Talk about them when you sit at home and when you walk along the road, when you lie down and when you get up. Tie them as symbols on your hands and bind them on your foreheads. Write them on the doorframes of your houses and on your gates."

Living in our age of information today, it may be difficult to grasp just how important oral tradition was for the Jews. Some conclude that memorizing could be unreliable or that there was a greater possibility for error. But when the 'oldies but goldies' songs are played on the radio, how quickly do the lyrics come back to mind? Right away, we find ourselves singing along. That demonstrates the power of memorization. I use to listen to the Beatles so much that it's hard to stump me on the lyrics some thirty years later. So it was with the entire community of Jews. Oral tradition was, in fact, self-correcting. If someone quoted a scripture inaccurately, there was someone listening who would quickly offer correction.

To a devout Jew, life revolved around learning the Scriptures and practicing them. Jesus told the Pharisees and the religious rulers of His day, "You diligently study the Scriptures because you think that by them you possess eternal life. These are the Scriptures that testify about me, yet you refuse to come to me to have life."[4]

Jesus punctuated the truth that the Scriptures pointed to Him! In fact, a study of every book in the Bible declares, foreshadows, or proclaims Jesus. He is the central theme of all Scripture written.

The Jewish Sacrifices for Atonement for Sins

Israel as a nation did not recognize Jesus as the Messiah when He came. One of the reasons for their unbelief was because they were looking for a ruler, a king, who would set up the kingdom for Israel, a government on earth from which He would rule the nations. Little did they understand that Jesus' *first* coming had to take care of the *sin* problem before He could one day restore the kingdom to Israel. They completely missed the prophecy in Daniel 9:26 that foretold that Messiah would be 'cut off' (or killed), but not for himself (or because of his own wrongdoing, but for the sins of the people).

God gave Moses the Ten Commandments and all of the Law. The Law was written for at least three reasons: (1) It showed Israel how to act in a holy manner; (2) the law showed them that *no one* was holy enough to keep all of the Law and (3) when they did sin, how to make restitution or atone for their sins. The Jews were well aware they had sins to be atoned for.

The Hebrew word for atonement is *"covering."* [5] They knew that "all things by the law [are] purged with blood; and without the shedding of blood, there is no remission of sins."[6] Why is that? Simple: a life for a life. But a covering or atonement for sin was actually instituted long before the Law was given. When? Surprisingly enough, immediately after the fall of man.

God Himself instituted the first blood sacrifice. When Adam and Eve sinned in the Garden of Eden, a crime had been committed, and someone had to pay. For the first time, they both felt fear and shame. They suddenly noticed they were naked. But hadn't they been naked all along? Why were they just now noticing? What was missing from their bodies? What had they been *covered* with?

You see, God is spirit,[7] and He created them in His image—spirit. God formed their body, gave them a soul, but the spirit enabled them to have perfect communion with Him. Adam and Eve were spiritual humans with a glorified body, just like we will have one day in paradise. God made it clear that they were free to eat anything in the Garden except the fruit of the tree of the knowledge of good and evil. God also made the consequence for disobedience known, saying, "for in *the day* that thou eatest thereof thou shalt surely die."[8] "The day" means 'in that very day,' or immediately, they would die. But Adam and Eve lived hundreds of years longer. So, what died? The spirit. Their spiritual covering had vanished, or 'died,' breaking that intimate connection with God. [9]

Remember what Adam and Eve did when they first realized they were naked and ashamed? They sewed fig leaves together and made *coverings* for themselves. It truly was the first act of religion, which is always man's attempt to cover himself by the work of his own hands. But their own works were futile. That's why God Himself stepped in.

With the fall of Adam and Eve, sin entered the world, and sadly, the sin nature within all humankind has been part of our history and dilemma. But a remedy was waiting in the wings. "Looking back you realize what God was doing. He was teaching them that by the shedding of blood on another tree in another garden, they would finally be covered—'spiritually.' " [10] God had a plan from before the foundation of the world to free us from our sin and eventually return us to a state of paradise with our redeemed glorified bodies.

Most scholars believe that the animal God used for

their sacrifice was a *lamb*. Why? Because Abel, who was a shepherd, offered the firstling from his flock, which in all probability was a lamb. Where would Abel have learned that practice except from his parents? And you know what happened after that. Cain offered fruits from the soil as an offering to the Lord, but the Lord favored Abel's offering. Because of Cain's jealousy, he murdered his brother Abel, whose death was a foreshadowing of Jesus'. But then, it would be Satan, the god of this world, who would turn his jealous anger towards the Son of God, in effect 'murdering' Him, hoping to ruin God's plan of redemption.

How horrible the sight must have been as Adam and Eve stood by and watched a precious lamb, which had done no wrong, slain before their eyes. Watching in shock, it easily could have been the first time they had ever seen blood. Now it spewed out as the animal grew limp and finally lifeless. Tears must have flowed as they realized that their wrongdoing had caused this hideous act. Then they had to watch as God Himself tore the skin from the animal's body to make a substitute covering for them. What a sad day it was as they wrestled with their guilt and shame.

Later on in Israel's history, the Passover was instituted by God and given to Moses. [11] It commemorated Israel's deliverance from the last plague against Egypt and their menacing Pharaoh—the death of the firstborn. In order to save the firstborn of Israel from the angel of death, Moses told them, as God had instructed him, to sacrifice a lamb without spot or blemish and take the blood of the lamb to cover the top of the doorpost, the sides, and the bottom (making the shape of a cross on their doors) so that the angel of death would pass over their dwelling sparing their firstborn. The blood of the lamb was the sign for death to 'pass over' them.

John the Baptist, upon seeing Jesus, exclaimed, "Behold! The Lamb of God who takes away the sins of the world!"[12] Peter said in his epistle, "For you know that it was not with perishable things such as silver or gold that you were redeemed from the empty way of life handed down to you from your forefathers, but with the precious blood of Christ, a lamb without blemish or defect."[13]

Jesus, our Passover Lamb, was slaughtered to atone for all sin and spare us from death! Only the perfect blood of God's Son could accomplish this salvation. All because God so loved the world He sent His only Son. The sin problem had to be taken care of before we could be considered the sons and daughters of God—the true brethren of Jesus now. Jesus' sacrificial blood has accomplished more than simply COVERING our sins; it has cleansed and washed away all our sins from within! And by believing in Him, we receive what Adam and Eve lost—*the Spirit of God!* The connection between God and man has been restored!

Back to this question: did Jesus *BECOME* sin, or was He the sin *OFFERING?*

The sacrificial lamb, one without spot or blemish, was used as the offering for sin.[14] The sins of the people were placed on the lamb by the high priest. What does it mean that the sins were 'placed on?' Did the lamb *become* sin? No. The lamb r*epresented* or *served as a substitute* for the payment of the people's sin. These are two entirely different grammatical concepts. It's really simple English. A lamb cannot sin or magically become or turn into sin, no more than Jesus magically turned into an actual lamb.

So what about 2 Corinthians 5:21 that says, "God made him who had no sin *to be* sin for us, so that in him we might become the righteousness of God"; and 1 Peter 2:24, which says, "Who his own self bare our sins in his own body on the tree that we, being dead to sins, should live unto righteousness: by whose stripes ye were healed"?

This verse cannot mean that Christ so took upon himself the sins of people that he became a sinner; it must mean that he put himself *in the place of* sinners, and bore that which those sins deserved. He was treated as if he had been a sinner, in order that we might be treated as if we had not sinned; that is, as if we were righteous. "There is no other way in which we can conceive that one bears the sins of another. They cannot be *literally* transferred to another; and all that can be meant is that he should take the consequences on himself, and suffer *as if he had* committed the transgressions himself."[15]

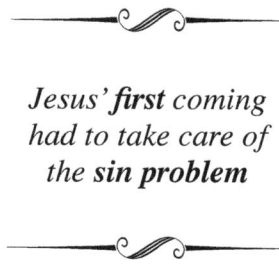

Jesus' first coming had to take care of the sin problem

No better example of this concept is seen than in the freeing of Barabbas by Pilate. The Roman custom was that, on certain holidays, one guilty prisoner was allowed to go free. Both Jesus and Barabbas were offered to the crowd and the people chose Barabbas. Think about these two men. The guilty was released from his debt of sin, while the innocent one took his place. Barabbas knew he was guilty and by law should have suffered death. He also knew that he had done nothing to merit such a gift.

Jesus is described as the suffering servant in Isaiah

53.[16] Throughout this prophecy about the Messiah's crucifixion and the spiritual meaning of the cross, notice how many times the phrase includes "borne," "carried," "took up," "upon," "laid on him," "bear," or "bore."

- Surely he *took up* our infirmities and *carried* our sorrows…
- The punishment that brought us peace was *upon* him.
- The Lord has *laid on him* the iniquity of us all.
- …though the Lord makes his life a guilt *offering*, he will see his offspring and prolong his days, and the will of the Lord will prosper in his hand.
- by his knowledge my righteous servant will justify many, and he will *bear* their iniquities.
- Therefore I will give him a portion among the great, and he will divide the spoils with the strong, because he poured out his life unto death, and was numbered with the transgressors. For he *bore* the sin of many, and made intercession for the transgressors.

Clarke's Commentary explains I Peter 2:24 succinctly: "The phrase 'bare our sins in his own body' means "bore the *punishment* due to our sins." In no other sense could Christ bear them. To say that they were so imputed to him as if they had been his own, and that the Father beheld him as blackened with imputed sin, is monstrous, if not blasphemous."[17]

Romans 3:25 states, "God presented him as a *sacrifice* of atonement, through faith in his blood" (emphasis added). The words 'sin offering' or 'offering for sin(s)' occurs hundreds of times throughout Scripture, but there is only <u>one</u> usage of "becoming sin," which is the verse that is used to teach that Jesus became sin (2 Cor. 5:21.) Wouldn't it make more sense to interpret the single verse in light of all the clear ones?

Romans 8:3–4: "For what the law was powerless to do in that it was weakened by the sinful nature, God did by sending his own Son in the *likeness* of sinful man to be a *sin offering*. And so he *condemned sin in sinful man*, in order that the righteous requirements of the law might be fulfilled in us" (emphasis added).

God did not condemn Jesus because He became sin. God condemned sin in sinful man. Jesus was not a sinful man; He was the offering for sinful man. Our sins were imputed to Him. The word *imputed* is a banking term that means to credit or make a deposit in an account. In other words, our account full of sins was transferred to His account. He didn't 'become' the account—He received the deposit.

Which do you believe now – that Jesus *became* sin or that Jesus became our sin *offering*?

To say that Jesus bore our sins in his own body means that He bore the punishment due for our sins

Even if you still insist on saying that Jesus became sin because he had to endure the separation from God on our behalf, it is virtually impossible to prove from scripture that God's eyes are too pure to look at sin—period.

A synopsis of the historical and cultural information of the times has added the following insight: daily learning and memorizing of the Scripture was highly valued, the rabbis were given the task of teaching the Scriptures and provoking memorization by often quoting the first and last verses, the Law required the sacrificial lamb as their atonement or covering for sins and that Jesus was and is our sacrificial lamb.

With this in mind, let's return to that day that Jesus hung on the cross and cried with a loud voice, *"My God, my God, why have you forsaken me?"*

CHAPTER 6

Dying Words: Failure or Fulfillment?

*Do not think that I have come to
abolish the Law or the Prophets;
I have not come to abolish them but to <u>fulfill them</u>.*
—JOHN 5:17, EMPHASIS ADDED

Dr. Charles Ryrie says that according to the laws of chance, it would require two hundred billion earths, populated with four billion people each, to come up with one person whose life could fulfill one hundred accurate prophecies without any errors in sequence. Yet the Scriptures record not one hundred, but over three hundred, prophecies that were fulfilled in Christ's first coming alone.

During the Passion Week, scores of scriptures were being fulfilled, as noted earlier from John's Gospel. John unequivocally reminded the reader that everything that was happening to Jesus during the crucifixion was so that Scripture could be fulfilled. Moreover, it was so from the beginning of His public ministry. Consider His early remarks in the synagogue:

"After being handed the scroll of Isaiah, He found the place where it was written: 'The Spirit of the Lord is upon me, because he has anointed me to preach the good news to the poor. He has sent me to proclaim freedom for the prisoners and recovery of sight to the blind, to release the oppressed, to proclaim the year of the Lord's favor.' Then He rolled up the scroll, gave it back to the attendant, and sat down. The eyes of everyone in the synagogue were fastened on him, and He began by saying, '*Today, this scripture is fulfilled in your hearing.*' " [1]

*"The Father who sent me commanded me **what to say** and **how to say it**. So **whatever I say is just what the Father has told me to say**"* (emphasis added).

Of all the scriptures He could have chosen that day, He carefully selected these. His timing was perfect. The people listening that day knew He was reading from Isaiah however Jesus omitted the last phrase which adds "and the day of vengeance of our God." Why do you suppose He left that phrase out? Obviously because that day has not yet come—the vengeance of God is still future. He read just the part that was fulfilled before their very eyes and ears, and in so doing, He was declaring Himself to be the Anointed One, the Messiah! Those who understood the Messianic prophecy of Isaiah knew exactly what Jesus was alluding to—and they didn't like it one bit. So much so they wanted to throw Him off a cliff.

It is essential to grasp that everything Jesus did or said was to fulfill the Holy Scriptures from the beginning of His ministry to the his final breath. In fact, let's consider all of the sayings of Jesus during His crucifixion. Were these also fulfilling Scripture as He spoke them? If a dying man has enough strength and wits about him, his last words are probably chosen very carefully. Those are the ones that the living remember for the rest of their lives. So precisely what were Jesus' dying words from the cross, and how much importance do they carry?

1) *"Father, forgive them, for they know not what they do"* (Luke 23:34). Fulfillment of Isaiah 53:12: "For he bore [carried] the sin of many, and made intercession for the transgressors."
2) *"I tell you the truth, today you will be with me in*

paradise" (Luke 23:43). Fulfilled in Isaiah 53:11–12: "After the suffering of his soul, he will see the light of life and be satisfied; by his knowledge my righteous servant will justify many, and he will bear their iniquities. . . . And he will divide the spoils with the strong, because he poured out his life unto death, and was numbered with the transgressors."

3) *"Woman, behold your son" [to Mary]. And to the disciple [John], "Behold your mother"* (John 19:26–27). Here, Jesus was fulfilling one of the Ten Commandments to honor (respect, care for) His mother as stated in Deuteronomy 5:16. As the oldest son, He passed on His responsibility to someone He trusted and stood by Him to the end, John.

4) *"I thirst."* "Later, knowing that all was now completed, and so that the Scripture would be fulfilled, Jesus said, "I am thirsty" (John 19:28). This remark was the fulfillment of Psalm 69:21, where it says, "They put gall in my food and gave me vinegar for my thirst."

5) *"It is finished"* (John 19:30). To be discussed later.
6) *"Father, into your hands I commit my spirit"* (Luke 23:45). This was quoted exactly from Psalm 31:5: "Into your hands I commit my spirit; redeem me, O Lord, the God of truth."

All these words that Jesus spoke from the cross were obviously not random comments. Jesus declared: "For I did not speak of my own accord, but the Father who sent me commanded me *what to say* and *how to say it. So whatever I say is just what the Father has told me to say."* [2]

Read that again! Did Jesus mean *everything* He spoke was what the Father told Him to? And notice that the Father even told Him *how* to say it! Jesus reiterated this same truth when he said: "These words you hear are not my own; they belong to the Father who sent me." [3]

So, if Jesus always said exactly what the Father told Him to say and even how the Father wanted it to be said, then what about this cry from the cross, "My God, my God, why have you forsaken me?" Did the Father tell Him to say that and to say it with a loud voice?

If that's true, then why on earth would the Father tell Jesus to say that? This poses a dilemma. If the Father is telling him to say this loudly, then the Father is inarguably communicating with His Son, which would signify He had not abandoned him. If we dig a little deeper, there has to be a very good biblical explanation.

The treasure is about to be unearthed!

CHAPTER 7

THE CROSS FROM JESUS' POINT OF VIEW

"I am poured out like water,
and all my bones are out of joint.
My heart has turned to wax; it has melted within me."
PSALM 22:14

*H*ave you ever wondered what was going through Jesus' mind as He suffered on the cross besides grappling with excruciating pain? We know He asked forgiveness for His torturers so He felt compassion. He said He was thirsty. He was concerned for His mother's care. Jesus also experienced some type of joy that enabled Him to set His face like flint and courageously obey the Father's will to the end. But what else was He thinking or feeling? Did you know that some of his thoughts were written for us in Psalm 22?

Scholars and commentaries agree that this Psalm written by King David was always considered a Messianic Psalm by the Jews. Oddly enough, it opens with this cry: *"My God, my God, why hast thou forsaken me?"*

David is pouring out his heart to the Lord about his own sufferings, expressing his feelings of abandonment from God because as yet, God had not delivered him from his enemies. Most likely, we have all experienced 'silence' from God as we plead for deliverance. However, by verse 5, David turns his focus, not to his own plight, but to the One who will come and truly suffer. It is as if he is 'seeing' that day when his Lord will lay down His life as David begins to describe the crucifixion in detail as if Jesus Himself were actually speaking!

"But I am a *worm*[1] and not a man, scorned by men and despised by the people. All who see me mock me; they hurl insults, shaking their heads; 'he trusts in the Lord; let the Lord rescue him. Let him deliver him, since he delights in him.¹' "

The fulfillment of these inflammatory insults can be heard almost verbatim in Matthew 27:39–44: "Those who passed by hurled insults at Him, shaking their heads and saying, 'You who were going to destroy the temple and build it in three days, save yourself! Come down from the cross, if you are the Son of God!' In the same way, the chief priests, the teachers of the law, and the elders mocked him. 'He saved others,' they said, 'but he can't save himself! He's the king of Israel! Let him come down now from the cross, and we will believe in him. He trusts in God. Let God rescue him now if he wants him, for he said, 'I am the Son of God.' " Imagine—history written in reverse – right down to the exact comments that would be made at the foot of His cross!

In verses 14 and 15, you can almost feel Jesus' agony: "I am poured out like water, and all my bones are out of joint. My heart has turned to wax; it has melted away within me. My strength is dried up like a potsherd, and my tongue sticks to the roof of my mouth." Imagine the unspeakable ordeal that his body was suffering and the only thing he mentioned about his predicament was that he was thirsty. It's enough to break anyone's heart.

Crucifixion was originally invented by the Persians between 300-400 B.C and later 'perfected' by the Romans about 100 B.C. It was undeniably the most painful death ever invented by man and is where we get our term "excruciating." David wrote this psalm almost a thousand years before Christ was born and about four hundred years before crucifixion had even been invented!

"Dogs [Gentiles] have surrounded me; a band of evil men have encircled me; **THEY HAVE PIERCED MY HANDS AND MY FEET.** I can count all my bones; people stare and gloat over me. They divide my clothes among them and cast lots for my garment." [2]

David's hands or feet were not 'pierced' nor did anyone cast lots for his garments. This verse can be interpreted no other way except in light of the crucifixion of Jesus. David, by the Spirit, was seeing and foretelling what would happen to his Lord.

David said that he foresaw the Lord always in front of him and that his Lord would not experience decay, which alludes to the fact that Messiah would die. [3] Later, after the resurrection and ascension, Peter refers to David's prophecy as he explains the resurrection to the crowd of Israelites on the Day of Pentecost in Acts 2: 29-34:

"Brothers, I can speak confidently to you about our forefather David, that he both died and was buried, and his tomb is with us to this day. So then, because he was a prophet and knew that God had sworn to him with an oath to seat one of his descendants on his throne, David by foreseeing this, spoke about the resurrection of the Christ that he was neither abandoned to Hades, nor did his body experience decay. This Jesus, God raised up, and we are all witnesses of it. So then, exalted to the right hand of God, and having received the promise of the Holy Spirit from the Father, he has poured out what you both see and hear. For David did not ascend into heaven..."

Peter confirms that David was prophesying about the coming Messiah. Psalm 22 continues: "I will declare your name to my brothers; in the congregation I will praise you. You, who fear the Lord, praise him! All you descendants of Jacob honor him! Revere him, all you descendants of Israel!" [4]

Why is this praise written here? The crucifixion was taking place and those who loved him were devastated! Can you imagine following and devoting your life to Jesus for over three years, knowing that He was the one Israel had been waiting for—the Messiah? You were with Him when He healed the sick, raised the dead, cleansed the leper, and forgave sins. You heard Him teach the Scriptures with authority and predict events that would occur right before your very eyes.

Now you are hiding from fear, experiencing the nerve-wracking trauma of Jesus' arrest and bloody torture, and you witness (or hear of) His horrific crucifixion. Jesus of Nazareth, who had done no wrong, who was to be the hope of Israel, now hangs helplessly on a cross. This unexpected shock would attack your faith to the core. Would you question everything about Him? Would you imagine that you had been duped by a false prophet? The mental anguish and confusion would be overwhelming.

Jesus, knowing how His followers felt, brings forth this psalm loud and clear to comfort and later convince them that His sacrifice was just what the Father had planned! From Jesus' point of view, the next verse declares His Father's presence with Him as He hung on the cross:

"For he has NOT despised or disdained the suffering of the afflicted one; he has not hidden his face from him but has listened to his cry for help" (emphasis added).

There it is—in black and white—God did not hide His face from Him! Could it be any clearer? If the previous verses in the psalm foretold the events of the crucifixion, why not this verse as well?

Jesus was called "rabbi" (meaning "teacher") by His disciples and followers. If you will remember from chapter 4, rabbis would frequently quote the first line of a scriptural text, then the congregation of Jews would follow by quoting the rest of that section, and lastly, the rabbi would say the last verse to close. Unfortunately, we do not have the advantage of the tone of Jesus' voice when He speaks these words. No recording. No elaboration from the text.

We only know He said it loudly.

As a rabbi, is it possible that Jesus was quoting the first line of Psalm 22 in order for those Jews standing around to immediately call to memory this entire psalm? If so, why would Jesus want to evoke this particular psalm as He was dying?

The Roman guards standing around would not have understood the meaning of Jesus' cry, for they were not learned in the Scriptures; some nearby mistook His words as a call to Elijah. But devout, learned Jewish people would recognize this as a quote from David's Messianic Psalm. Perhaps even the learned Pharisees would have gasped if they were smart enough to recall the Psalm.

David wrote Psalm 22 almost a thousand years before Christ was born and about four hundred years before crucifixion had even been invented!

Continuing in Psalm 22, we see God's remarkable plan

of salvation through His Son's sacrifice and the coming exaltation and dominion over all the earth that will be given to Him!

"All the ends of the earth **will remember** [will remember what—that Jesus, as the Messiah, fulfilled these prophetic words] and **turn to the Lord**, and all the families of the nations **will bow down before him,** for dominion belongs to the Lord and he rules over the nations. All the rich of the earth will feast and worship; all who go down to the dust will **kneel before him**"[5]—those who cannot keep themselves alive (which is everyone).

They *will* remember and they *will* bow down. Paul unmistakably confirms the same—that because Jesus humbled Himself to the death on the cross that "God has highly exalted him and bestowed on him the name that is above every name, so that at the name of Jesus every knee should bow, in heaven and on earth and under the earth, and every tongue confess that Jesus Christ is Lord, to the glory of God the Father."[6] But that's not all . . .

"Posterity will serve him; future generations will be told about the Lord. They will proclaim *his* righteousness [through his blood] to a people yet unborn—[that is you and me!] for he has done *it.*"[7]

Fulfilled! Future generations have been told about the Lord and have served Him! You and I, who were yet unborn at the time, continue to proclaim Him today.

Now for the staggering truth about the last four words of this psalm – "he has done it." The word *done* is the Greek word *'ā·śāh*, which means "performed," "accomplished," or "finished." In the King James Version, you can see that the word *it* is in italics, indicating that the translators added it. The pronoun *he* should be *it*, so that the psalm closes with the words "for it is finished."

"It is finished!"

Go back to the cross that day. After Jesus cried out with a loud voice, "My God, my God, why hast thou forsaken me,?" His very next words were "It is finished."

He quoted the first and the last line of Psalm 22. As the rabbi, the teacher, Jesus was teaching and fulfilling Scripture as He was dying so that we might believe! He was not asking why he had been abandoned. He was not the misunderstood martyr. God had not turned His back on His Son. Jesus said these words with a loud voice to fulfill the Scripture that told all of these things would happen – and that His Father had not abandoned Him as his accusers had said.

Jesus began His ministry with "It is written" to the devil in the wilderness and closed His earthly mission with his final breath declaring "It is written"!

After He rose from the dead, in His new resurrected body, He still taught "it is written" to the two men on the road to Emmaus when he said, "How foolish you are, and how slow of heart to believe all that the prophets have spoken! Did not the Christ have to suffer these things and then enter his glory?" And beginning with Moses and all the prophets, he explained to them what was said in all the scriptures concerning himself."[8]

For he has NOT despised or disdained the suffering of the afflicted one; he has not hidden his face from him but has listened to his cry for help.

He explained to them what was said in all the scriptures concerning Himself. In my estimation, He could have even referred to Psalm 22 as He taught them. Jesus Christ is the Word in the flesh.[9] He knew the Word, He declared the Word, and He fulfilled the Word. He is the embodiment of "it is written"!

John, in his Gospel, inserts a 'footnote,' of sorts when he explains, "At first his disciples did not understand all this. Only after Jesus was glorified did they realize that these things had been written about him and that these things had been done to him."[10]

Oh how I would love to know all that Jesus taught His disciples and other followers during those forty days after His resurrection and before His ascension! After "it is finished," Jesus finished and restored their faith because He is the author and finisher of faith! Any traces of doubt that Jesus was indeed the Messiah, the Son of God, were completely erased. So much so, that every one of the twelve disciples died as martyrs for His name, except for John who was exiled to the Isle of Patmos.

How about you? Are there any traces of doubt left that Jesus is the Messiah, the Son of God, and that He did exactly what the Father sent Him to do, down to His very last words?

Did God forsake Jesus on the cross? Absolutely not. Scripture has spoken.

SUMMARY

*I am the way and the truth and the life.
No one comes to the Father except through me.*
—John 14:6

*Now Jesus did many other signs in the
presence of the disciples,
which are not written in this book; but these are written
so that you may believe that Jesus is the Christ,
the Son of God,
and that by believing you may have life in his name."*
John 20:31, 31

*S*urely, if you are a seeker of the truth, there is nothing to do but stand in awe of our Lord and Savior, Jesus Christ. No wonder He alone is worthy to be called the Lamb of God, our Savior, Master and Lord. And He calls Himself our *friend.* And what a friend we have in

Him.

Jesus fulfilled every scripture foretold about Him. No other founder of any religion has had so much criteria and prophetic detail told of him thousands of years before he came. And there are still hundreds of scriptures *yet* to be fulfilled, and since God is faithful to His Word, you can bet they will be!

"And just as it is appointed for man to die once, and after that comes judgment, so Christ, having been offered once to bear the sins of many, will appear a second time, not to deal with sin, but to save (rescue) those who are eagerly waiting for him."[1]

The Lord Jesus Himself will once again come to earth, but not to be born in a manger or to be despised, rejected, betrayed, and crucified. Since that awful day on the cross, Jesus is risen and alive right now. If He fulfilled all the scriptures about his birth, ministry, death, resurrection, and ascension, then surely He is coming again in glory to set up His kingdom here on earth. Only those who have believed in Him will inherit eternal life, and those who been faithful to His words will reign with Him. There is no other truth.

If you want a friend like Jesus but have never asked

SUMMARY

Him to be the Lord over your life, to forgive you of your sins, to save you from darkness and death, why not now? "Behold, NOW is the day of salvation!" If you do believe that Jesus is the Son of God and the only Way, the only Truth and the only way to have Life, what have you got to lose? He paid the price for sin so that you don't have to – it's a free gift to you. If He was a false Messiah, you still haven't lost anything. No one or nothing else promises eternal life. But if you don't reach out to Jesus, then you may never know the joy of His friendship and eternal life, peace and joy. That would be sad indeed.

Jesus wants a relationship with you forever. He loves you so much. He wants you to know Him, trust Him, confide in Him, and simply love Him back. After He ascended from earth into the heavens to sit at the right hand of God, He secured a gift for us—the gift of the Holy Spirit, which comes to live within us. This is how we communicate with Him. He has restored the spirit that Adam and Eve lost.

Remember that Jesus prayed for YOU the night before He was crucified? *"I do not ask for these only [the eleven disciples with Him], but also for **those who will believe in me** through their word, that they may all be one, just as you, Father, are in me, and I in you, that they also may be in us, so that the world may believe that you have sent me."*[2]

Jesus prayed that you would one day believe in Him. Just as any Broadway show needs a good director, any sports team needs a good coach, those in trouble need a counselor, or friends need one another, certainly we need a director, a coach, a partner, a counselor, a FRIEND, in this life. No other will do. There is no one so faithful.

Jesus will never ever leave you or ever, ever forsake you. It is written, "God has said, 'Never will I leave you; never will I forsake you.' So we say with confidence, 'The Lord is my helper; I will not be afraid. What can mere mortals do to me?' "[3]

Choose life. Choose Jesus.

"And lo, I am with you always, even unto the end of the age."[4]
"Now may the God of peace who brought again from the dead our Lord Jesus, the great shepherd of the sheep, by the blood of the eternal covenant, equip you with everything good that you may do his will, working in us that which is pleasing in his sight, through Jesus Christ, to whom be glory forever and ever. Amen." [5]

END NOTES

Bibles:

The New International Version, Zondervan Publishing House, Grand Rapids, MI, 1985

The Companion Bible, King James Version, Zondervan Publishing House, Grand Rapids, MI, 1974

Biblia.com, Bible Study Online, Logos Bible Software, trademarks of Logos Research Systems, Inc., d.b.a. Logos Bible Software. 1992

Concordance:

Strong's Exhaustive Concordance, http://www.biblestudytools.com/concordances/strongs-exhaustive-concordance/ http://www.salemwebnetwork.com, 1999.

Chapter One

1. Matthew 16:25, KJV.
2. John 16:12–14, KJV, emphasis added.
3. II Timothy 2:15, KJV, emphasis added.
4. James 3:1
5. II Peter 1:20, 21, KJV.
6. A "Jot" is the tiniest letter of the Hebrew alphabet and a "tittle" is a decorative mark similar to our comma.

Chapter Two

1. "Why did Jesus Cry Out, 'My God, My God, why have you forsaken Me?'" Accessed February 10, 2013. http://www.carm.org/questions/about-jesus/why-did-jesus-cry-out-my-god-my-god-why-have-you-forsaken-me
2. Got Questions.org. "Why did Jesus say, "My God, my God, why have you forsaken me?" Accessed February 10, 2013. http://www.gotquestions.org/forsaken-me.html
3. Matthew 26: 53
4. John 16: 32, emphasis added.
5. I Peter 2:23
6. Job 42:7, emphasis added.
7. Exodus 20:7, KJV.
8. Strong's Concordance #7722.
9. Matthew 26:39, KJV.
10. John 17:20, 21, KJV.

Chapter Three

1. Strong's Concordance #2316-- theos: 2a) God the Father; 3) spoken of the only and true God; 3a) refers to the things of God
2. John 20 17, KJV.
3. Dictionary.com; http://dictionary.reference.com/browse/why?s=t
4. John 12 27
5. John16:28
6. John 14 31
7. John 18 11
8. John 18 4
9. Luke 9: 28, 29, 51
10. Matthew 14:31
11. Luke 22:31
12. I Peter 1:19; 2:22; Acts 3:14; II Cor. 5:21; Hebrews 4:15; 7:26; I John 3:5
13. Deut. 31: 6 & 8
14. Joshua 1:5
15. Hebrews 5:7
16. John 11:41
17. Luke 23:46

Chapter Four

1. See Matthew 4:1-11; Mark 1:12, 13; Luke 4:1-13
2. John 13:18, 19, emphasis added.
3. John 14:29, emphasis added.

4. John 15:25, emphasis added.
5. John 19:23, 24, emphasis added.
6. John 19: 28, emphasis added.
7. John 19: 34 – 36, emphasis added.
8. Psalm 34:20
9. Zechariah 12:10
10. Isaiah 53:12
11. Luke 22:36 & 37, emphasis added.

For more elucidation on prophecies fulfilled by Jesus, see "A Rabbi Looks at Jesus of Nazareth," by Jonathan Bernis, pages 51-56.

Chapter Five

1. Dr. Chuck Missler, www.khouse.org "Learn the Bible in 24 Hours"
2. According to an ancient document called the *Letter of Aristeas*, it is believed that 70 to 72 Jewish scholars were commissioned during the reign of Ptolemy Philadelphus to carry out the task of translation. The term "Septuagint" means seventy in Latin, and the text is so named to the credit of these 70 scholars. http://www.septuagint.net/
3. Blair Kasfeldt, http://suite101.com/article/jewish-education-in-the-ancient-world-and-memory-of-scripture-a352476
4. John 5:39–40
5. Atonement - Bible Dictionary: http://topicalbible.org/a/

END NOTES

atonement.htm - The English word atonement originally denoted the reconciliation of parties previously at variance. It is used in the Old Testament to translate a Hebrew word which means a covering; implying that by a Divine propitiation the sinner is covered from the just anger of God. This is actually put into effect by the death of Christ; while the ceremonial offerings of the Jewish church only secured from impending temporal judgments, and typified the blood of Jesus Christ which "cleanses us from all sin."

6. Hebrews 9:22
7. Luke 4:24
8. Genesis 2:17, KJV, emphasis added.
9. https://net.bible.org/#!bible/Genesis+2:9 NET Bible Text Note. "Or 'in the very day, as soon as.' The imperfect verb form here has the nuance of the specific future because it is introduced with the temporal clause, "when you eat…you will die." That certainty is underscored with the infinitive absolute, "you will *surely* die."
10. Dr. Chuck Missler. www.khouse.org "Learn the Bible in 24 Hours," page 21
11. Leviticus 4, 6, 8, 16 & Exodus 12
12. John 1:29
13. I Peter 1:18, 19
14. See Leviticus 4:29; 5:9; 8:14; 16:11, 25; Numbers 28:22; 29:11 for a few examples of the words "sin offering."
15. Barnes' Notes on the Bible; http://bible.cc/1_peter/2-24.htm, emphasis mine.

16. Isaiah 53. Emphasis added.
17. Clarke's Commentary on the Bible

Chapter Six
1. Luke 4:17-21, emphasis added.
2. John 12:49, emphasis added.
3. John 14:24

Chapter Seven
1. "The term 'worm', *tolah*, also means "scarlet" (it is rendered "crimson"38 times). Scarlet dye was made from a particular worm – Cermes vermilio. The Cermes vermilio pierces the thin bark of twigs to suck the sap, from which it prepares a waxy scale to protect its soft body. The red dye is in this scale. When reproducing, the female climbs a tree where it bears its eggs; the larvae hatch and feed on the body of the worm. It literally gives its life. A crimson stain is left on the branch. When the scarlet spot dries out, in 3 days (!) it changes to white. See Isaiah 1:18." Dr. Chuck Missler, Personal UPDATE; News Journal of Koinonia House, page 7.
2. Psalm 22:16-18, emphasis added.
3. Psalm 16:10.
4. Psalm 22:22, 23.
5. Psalm 22:27-31, emphasis added.
6. Philippians 2:9-11; quoted from Isaiah 45:23.
7. Psalm 22:30, 31

END NOTES

8. Luke 24:25–27
9. John 1:1.
10. John 12:16
11. Psalm 22:30, 31.

Summary

1. Hebrews 9:27,28
2. John 18:20
3. Hebrews 13:5 & 6
4. Matthew 28:20
5. Hebrews 13:20,21

www.ingramcontent.com/pod-product-compliance
Ingram Content Group UK Ltd.
Pitfield, Milton Keynes, MK11 3LW, UK
UKHW041950230426
12048UKWH00008B/244